T0197611

GOD'S
Great Big Love

MARCIA SHERIFF

WestBow Press books may be ordered through booksellers or by contacting:

WestBow Press
A Division of Thomas Nelson & Zondervan
1663 Liberty Drive
Bloomington, IN 47403
www.westbowpress.com
844-714-3454

Because of the dynamic nature of the Internet, any web addresses or links contained in this book may have changed since publication and may no longer be valid. The views expressed in this work are solely those of the author and do not necessarily reflect the views of the publisher, and the publisher hereby disclaims any responsibility for them.

Any people depicted in stock imagery provided by Thinkstock are models, and such images are being used for illustrative purposes only.

Certain stock imagery © Thinkstock.

Cover photograph by Jason Clements.
Page one: photograph by Marcia Sheriff. The bald eagle was photographed by Brad McClure.
Pages 2-7, 10, 13, 16, 18, and 20-21 Copyright Kevin Barber with Barber Photography
Pages 9 and 17 Copyright Kindra Barber with Barber Photography.
Pages 11-12, 14-15, and 19 Stock Photography from ThinkStock.
Page 8: Photograph taken by Cristi Rittgers with Lemon Tree Photography.

Psalm 19:1, Proverbs 17:17, and John 3:16 scripture quotations taken from The Holy Bible, English Standard Version® (ESV®), copyright © 2001 by Crossway, a publishing ministry of Good News Publishers. Used by permission. All rights reserved.

Psalm 23:1 Scripture quotation taken from the Holy Bible, New International Reader's Version®, NIrV® Copyright © 1995, 1996, 1998 by Biblica, Inc.™ Used by permission of Zondervan. www.zondervan.com The "NIrV" and "New International Reader's Version" are trademarks registered in the United States Patent and Trademark Office by Biblica, Inc.™

Psalm 135:3 scripture quotation taken from the New American Standard Bible®, Copyright © 1960, 1962, 1963, 1968, 1971, 1972, 1973, 1975, 1977, 1995 by The Lockman Foundation. Used by permission." (www.Lockman.org)

Jeremiah 31:13 scripture quotation taken from the New Century Version. Copyright © 2005 by Thomas Nelson, Inc. Used by permission. All rights reserved.

ISBN: 978-1-4497-9288-6 (sc)
ISBN: 978-1-4497-9287-9 (e)

Library of Congress Control Number: 2013907988

Print information available on the last page.

WestBow Press rev. date: 06/29/2021

WESTBOW
PRESS®
A DIVISION OF THOMAS NELSON
& ZONDERVAN

God's handiwork is painted
across the great big sky.

He made us and loves us,
so we lift his name on high.

His marvelous creation can be seen everywhere.

When we want to **thank** him, we can go to him in **prayer**.

"The heavens declare the glory of God and the sky above proclaims his handiwork."

Psalm 19:1

God made many beautiful
and thoughtful designs.

He made wonderful patterns
and orderly lines.

God enjoys the
lovely praises we sing.

We give him the glory for everything!

"Praise the Lord, for the Lord is good; sing praises to his name for it is lovely."

Psalm 135:3

God gives us a family
that is just right,

To **love** us, **care** for us,
and **hug** us real tight.

God gives us
good friends
to share life together

To laugh with,
play with,
and love us forever!

"A friend loves at all times…"
Proverbs 17:17

God **protects** us and **cares** for us too.

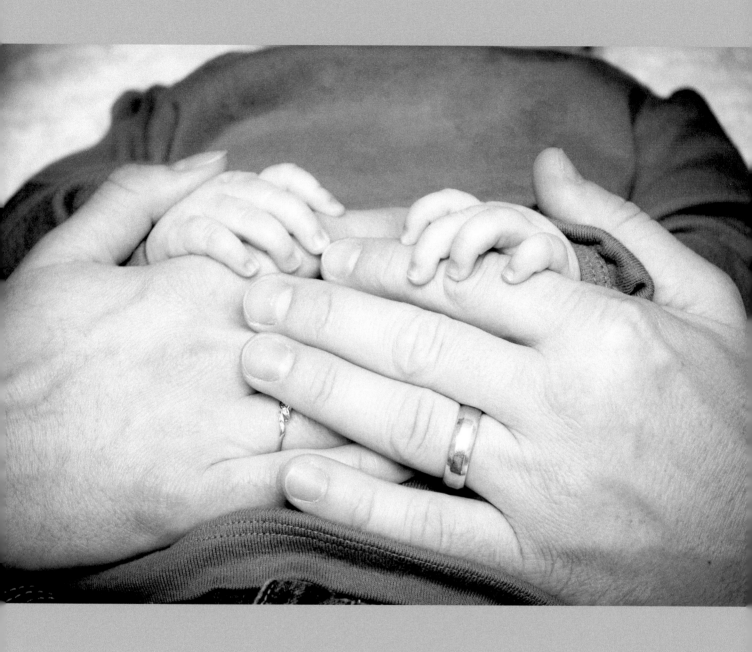

He **always** knows
the **right** things to do.

God can be trusted
to meet every need.

We should **love** others and **follow** His lead.

"The Lord is my shepherd. He gives me everything I need."
Psalm 23:1

Nothing separates us from
his love,
so deep.

God cares for us,
like a shepherd to his sheep.

When things go **wrong**
or we have a **bad day,**

God reassures us
that he's **here to stay!**

"...I will give them comfort
and joy instead of sadness."

Jeremiah 31:13

God's love
is a gift and
one-of-a-kind.

His goodness
and grace are
easy to find.

God is in our hearts
and will never leave.

He is our hope

and by faith we believe.

"For God so loved the world, that he gave his only Son, that whoever believes in him should not perish but have eternal life."

John 3:16

Printed in the United States
by Baker & Taylor Publisher Services